Beauty of
California

Beauty of
California

Text: Paul M. Lewis
Concept & Design: Robert D. Shangle

First Printing January, 1989
Published by LTA Publishing Company
1425 S.E. 18th Avenue, Portland, Oregon 97214
Robert D. Shangle, Publisher

"Learn about America in a beautiful way."

Library of Congress Cataloging-in-Publication Data
Beauty of California
/text, Paul M. Lewis; concept & design, Robert D. Shangle.
　　　　p.　　　cm.
ISBN 0-917630-71-8; $19.95. — ISBN 0-917630-42-4 (pbk.); $9.95
　　1. California — Description and travel — 1981 — Views.
I. Shangle, Robert D. II. Title
F862.L55　1989
917.94'0453 — dc19　　　　　　　　　　　　　　　88-37210
　　　　　　　　　　　　　　　　　　　　　　CIP

Copyright © 1989 by LTA Publishing Company
Printed in Hong Kong by Beauty of the Americas Printing Company
Offices: Seattle, Washington; Portland, Oregon; Hong Kong

Contents

Introduction

This book is only a sample, but an affectionate sample, of California's uncountable bedazzlements. An assortment of photographic artists have contributed some exquisite portraits from settings all over this big, photogenic state. My accompanying text, it is hoped, will supply enough background commentary so that the words and pictures, taken together, will contribute to your understanding of, and admiration for, a very complex and exceptional part of the United States.

Some say that the two halves of California, northern and southern, are like two separate kingdoms. The people who live in these respective areas probably do see their needs and interests in different lights. The out-and-out partisans may even go so far as to give legitimacy to that imaginary border between the two parts of the state — somewhere around Yosemite on the east, Merced in the center, and the Monterey Bay country on the coast. And in truth there are some striking differences. The farther away from the state's middle you get, north *or* south, the greater are the divergencies not only in climate and topography, but also in attitudes and goals.

It is not our purpose in putting together this book to take sides in the hassle over the differences between the two sections. Widely disparate ways of life are inevitable in a state that reaches from deep into the temperate zone down into the subtropical. Then there's the obvious fact that California, now, is the most populous state. As the numbers of persons increase, so do the points of view. And if there is a real philosophic parting of the ways, it is connected with numbers.

The north, with the lighter population, greener mountains, and more water, seems to want the status quo. To some that means keeping southern

Californians and others out of their paradise and putting a lock on the resources of the north. Southerners, on the other hand, have long been at work manipulating and changing the deserts, mountains, canyons and coastline of their half to accommodate the millions to whom southern California has meant the promised land. Southern Californians are accustomed to re-creating nature in their image of her, wrestling from the land the concessions that have made possible the great cities and the agricultural productivity of the south.

Lately, the signals have been on the side of a slowdown, but southern California has for decades equated growth with progress, the *sine quo non* of human happiness. Now that environmental awareness is part of the national consciousness, even the most ardent chamber-of-commerce types are coming around to the idea that continued population expansion may soon put a limit on the benefits of living in California.

Whatever the eventual direction California takes in the near and far future, I leave the business of prophetic vision up to those seers who have had more success than I in figuring out what's ahead. The California of today is what this book is all about; some of it is subtle and some is showy. And if the pictures say anything, they remind us of how very careful we must be to preserve the beauty they reflect. Whatever is lost by alteration or destruction diminishes the lives of Californians yet to come.

P.M.L.

Northern California

Extreme northern California has more affinity with Oregon and Washington than it does with the rest of California. Its green beauty, variety of mountainous terrains, and weather patterns make it an actual, if not a political, part of the Northwest. The southern Cascades push down along the eastern side and the Coast Range presents a solid barrier in the west. The two great chains have no definite dividing line in the far north of the state, merging into one great mass of mountain wilderness as far south as Red Bluff, at the head of the Central Valley.

The north coast has the generally mild climate that is distinctive to the Pacific West coastal states north into Washington (see The Coast). The inland areas of northern California have more pronounced seasonal variations, the summers being quite warm and the winters definitely wintry, although snows are infrequent except in the mountains. The southern Cascades and northern Sierras receive heavy snows in winter, but in summer, the Sierras, especially, have many warm days, which make them attractive for camping, hiking, and other recreational pursuits.

A little south of the Oregon border is a wilderness area comprising the Marble, Trinity, Salmon and Scott mountain systems. Far less developed than the popular Sierras to the southeast, these mountains can be more attractive to the nature lover because of their uncrowded accessibility and the comparative ease with which the high country can be reached. The Trinity Alps resemble the Sierras in the brusque thrust of their granite peaks, but they are closer-knit, so trails into them are shorter. Their closeness to the coast gives them more streams and lusher vegetation than the Sierras. The Trinity canyons are warm, like the Sacramento Valley, and the high wilderness is cooled by coastal winds and moisture. The Marble Mountains, a little to the northwest, are especially attractive to hikers. Their many scenic trails go by lakes and through forests of pine, hemlock, fir, and spruce. It is even possible to pack in on horseback, a preferred method for visiting the interior.

These northern mountains had their version of the Gold Rush, and although it was on a smaller scale than the frantic activity in the Sierra foothills to the south, there are still some testimonials to the wild and wooly days of that period. Towns, such as Shasta and Weaverville, contain buildings, mines, and other relics of the gold-rush times.

A little east of Interstate 5 in this same area stands the enormous Mt. Shasta, more than 14,100 feet high and containing five glaciers. Its heavy snows give skiers, in some years, a year-round season on its slopes.

About 45 miles southeast of Redding is Lassen Volcanic National Park. Lassen and the surrounding area offers evidence of 20th-century volcanic activity. The mountain blew up in 1915, sending lava, mud, and rocks into the valleys around it. Some of the devastated area has changed little since that time. The lava looks "new" and the trees killed by thermal activity litter the terrain. The heart of the Lassen country is open only by trail, but all of the park is within a day's hiking distance of a road. The Lassen Peak Road goes around a part of the park and affords a panoramic view of the volcano's effects on the area in addition to the sight of Mt. Shasta, the far-off Sierras, and the Coast Range.

The northeast corner contains some unusual geology, recreational lakes, and the Warner Mountains, whose heights are designated as wilderness. This area offers about the most in solitude that is possible in California. The Warners rise gradually in the west and break off abruptly on the eastern side. The South Warner Wilderness can be explored by hiking a 24-mile trail that lies partly along the summit of the range, then drops into rocky lowlands and meadows of wildflowers. Some side trails lead from the main trail to lakes and creeks where trout fishing is good.

A few miles to the southwest, the Feather River rises on the west slope of the Sierras and flows south through a rocky mountain and canyon country before joining the Sacramento River, about 100 miles away. The Feather, named by a Spanish explorer for the feathers he saw floating in the lower river during the band-tailed pigeon migration, is formed by three forks. An excellent view of the Feather River Canyon country is afforded by State Highway 70, which links the Central Valley to the Sierra. This is another former mining area and some roads from the main highway lead off into old mining settlements. Oroville, on the same highway, is 75 miles north of Sacramento and is considered the gateway to the Feather River country. It began as a rough gold mining town where great numbers of Chinese were employed to work the mines. Oroville has a Chinese temple, built in 1863. The temple is now a museum reflecting the Oriental culture of the town's Chinese population in the 1870s.

A few miles northeast of Oroville, storing the waters of the Feather River, is Oroville Dam, the highest landfill embankment in the world. The Oroville Lake, created by the dam, offers 167 miles of recreational shoreline. Just east of Lake Oroville is a 15,000-acre preserve called Feather Falls Scenic Area, named for its 640-foot falls. Much of the canyon area here is so rugged as to be inaccessible.

California's Central Valley is, of course, agricultural. Fruit orchards, vineyards, and staple crops are the mainstay of the valley's economy. In the northern, or Sacramento — half of the Central Valley, the cities of Sacramento and Stockton have, in recent times, become inland ports, thereby offering ocean access to the valley's products. The communities of the Sacramento Valley began during the Gold Rush days. Later, the valley's economy was developed along agricultural lines, and, at first, grain was the most important product. When irrigation was introduced and farm holdings became smaller, orchards, citrus groves, rice, and sugar beets surpassed grain in importance to the region. These crops are still the primary agricultural concerns of the Sacramento Valley.

The big Sacramento is almost a wild river until it gets within about 50 miles of its namesake city. Although it runs through lowlands from Red Bluff to the south, its current is strong and several species of waterfowl live on its waters and along its banks. Overlapping salmon and trout migrations make fishing a year-round sport. One of the most interesting towns along the northern river is Red Bluff, where many Victorian homes and stores of the Gold Rush era remain.

Within the rough ellipse formed by the cities of Sacramento, Stockton, and Pittsburg is the interesting Delta area, where the Sacramento, San Joaquin, and Mokelumne rivers meet and flow into the San Francisco Bay. They form a complicated network of channels and waterways, with expanses of muddy land in between. The land was once like an everglade, heavily forested with oak and pine, but the forests were cut to fuel early steamboats. The water lands have since then made money for asparagus and fruit farmers. The deep Delta channels are busy, both as commercial waterways and as routes for pleasure boats. Striped bass, salmon, sturgeon, catfish and shad provide exciting sport fishing for the Delta area.

South of Sacramento is the San Joaquin half of the Central Valley. This area developed agriculturally much later than the upper valley. Most of the population and commercial growth here have come after World War II. Fresno and Lodi are now centers of wine districts, where grapes are brought to peak-sugar content by the long, warm summers, producing dessert wines. Strung along State Highway 99, the highway which connects the cities of the San Joaquin Valley, are state parks, campsites, and recreation areas developed around lakes.

Southern California

When we think of Southern California, the first name that pops into the mind is usually "Los Angeles," a city that personifies not only the topography and climate of the southern half, but also the philosophy that has made "biggest," "best," and "most" the special qualities that have drawn so many people to this metropolis and made Southern California a leader in so many fields of human endeavor. Los Angeles seems more like a nation than a city. Its prodigal use of lateral space has stretched it out to the point where it is as big in area as the state of Rhode Island.

Los Angeles creates the pattern that makes southern California a unique place in the world. The 100 communities that make up the giant city are quite varied in topography, traditions, and philosophical values. The southern California state of mind has been nurtured here — this is the belief that anything is possible, a belief whose physical manifestation has made the Los Angeles way of life feasible. Some of these man-made marvels that come quickly to mind are the colossal pipelines that carry water over great distances to the city; the great power dams that supply it with electricity; the tangle of freeways that provide rapid movement within the city.

Leaving aside the man-made extravaganzas, we can see that nature has dealt lavishly with the Los Angeles area. It is blessed with an awesome variety of landscapes, including mountain ranges (Santa Monica, San Gabriel), a lush valley (San Fernando) until recently an important agricultural area, canyons, plains, and of course a long coastline with many fine, sandy beaches. The city's Griffith Park, just west of the Santa Monica Mountains, is the largest city park in the country. Beverly Hills and the Hollywood Hills are like introductions to the mountains that border the city to the north and east.

Coming down to the edge of Los Angeles, the San Gabriel Mountains separate the city from the desert to the north. The San Bernardino range, to the east, provides another barrier between city and desert land. The San Gabriels, part of the Coast Range, rise up from near the sea and stretch over to the Mojave Desert. Some of the peaks rise more than 10,000 feet and include, among others, Mt. Wilson, Mt. San Antonio — "Old Baldy" — and Big Pines. The San Gabriels, because of their proximity to Los Angeles, offer a handy mountain retreat for Angelenos. As with all mountain country, the best part is reached and seen only by trail. The front ranges of the San Gabriels are lavishly endowed with streams, waterfalls, gorges, and woodlands, all easily reached on short trails. The Angeles Crest Highway (State 2) runs along much of the San Gabriel Range.

The San Bernardinos are the highest range on the edge of Los Angeles. Mt. San Gorgonio is 11,500 feet and many other peaks are well over 10,000. State Highway 18, called "Rim of the World Drive," threads its way over the range, sometimes reaching up beyond 7,000 feet and passing lakes, ski areas, and resorts.

Next to the San Bernardinos, to the southeast, are the San Jacinto Mountains, small in area, but a tall and cool oasis between the warm wheat and orchard country of the San Jacinto Valley on the west and the hot Coachella Valley desert to the east. The San Jacintos rise gradually from south to north, dropping in sudden and spectactular fashion after reaching nearly 11,000 feet at San Jacinto Peak.

The southeast desert country east of the San Jacintos is celebrated for year-round sunshine and dry climate. It has become a resort area par excellence, and its foremost city, Palm Springs, is no longer, as it once was, the exclusive playground of the wealthy and famous. The steep San Jacinto Mountains provide Palm Springs with cool afternoon shade in the summer. Close to town are some beautiful and historic canyons: Palm, Andreas, Murray, and Fern. The Agua Caliente Indians have long lived in these valleys; they still own this canyonland which provides palm groves as a cool retreat from the hot desert.

14

The Coachella Valley, spreading out east and south from Palm Springs, is, for the most part, rich farmland wrested from the desert by irrigation. It is officially part of the Colorado Desert, to the east and south, and much of it is below sea level. Many kinds of fruit and vegetables are grown here, and the whole valley, irrigated or otherwise, supports a great variety of animal and plant life. Indio, in about mid-valley, is the center of date-growing activity — groves of date palms are very much a part of this region which gives reason for the Indio National Date Festival. The land of the southern part of the valley also yields such crops as cotton, vegetables, wine grapes, and citrus fruits. The valley ends at the salty Salton Sea, where the desert landscape, again, dominates. South of the Salton Sea, all the way to the border, is a still larger irrigated area that is really the same valley. But this region's prodigious agricultural performance has entitled it to an impressive label that sets it very much apart. This is the Imperial Valley, the champion crop-grower of the world.

East of these desert valleys, which are no longer "pure" desert because of man's alterations, is a preserve of high desert land, unaltered in any way by man. This is the Joshua Tree National Monument, east of Palm Springs and between the great Colorado and Mojave deserts. Because this is high desert, the ambience is different from that of the great lowland deserts around it. The weather is milder — 70 to 90 degrees in the winter. Its vegetation includes, besides the Joshua tree itself, cactus, the yucca tree, and thorny ocotillo shrub. And in the spring when there is enough rain, the Monument is covered with wildflowers. Primitive man is believed to have lived in this high desert as long as enough water was available. Some gold prospecting was done here in the 1860s, and some mine shafts and mills are still in evidence.

The Joshua Tree grows at 3,000- to 5,000-foot elevations in the preserve, part of which includes the Little San Bernardino Mountains. The tree is a spectacular plant limited to the southwestern deserts. It grows as high as 40 feet, in a twisted configuration, and with its upstretched branches appears to adopt a prayerful attitude. Thereby the name, Joshua tree, supposed to have been applied by the Mormons. The northern gateway and headquarters for the Monument is the town of Twentynine Palms, celebrated in song as the home of the lady with all those Cadillacs.

The Salton Sea, the divider between the Coachella and Imperial valleys, is an interesting body of water created by natural forces. The Sea is saltier than the oceans. The basin, holding it, received its waters in 1905, when the flooding Colorado River donated several billion gallons. The Salton is below sea level, has good roads around it, and resorts and recreational facilities. The area contains hot springs, Indian petroglyphs, old shell deposits, and dramatic canyons with deep, colored rock walls. Serious rock hunters could hardly find a better place for their activities.

On the eastern edge of San Diego's back country is the Anza-Borrego Desert State Park. The park extends about 50 miles north and south, reaching to the Mexican border. Its terrain varies from very low elevations to very high ones — 100 feet below sea level, where it touches the Salton Sea, to 6,000 feet above, with its highest mountain. It is by far the biggest preserve in the California system, and, except for Borrego Valley in the north, is one of the last unaltered deserts in the state. Its wastelands have a severe aspect, but it has many kinds of landscapes, from barren, clayey gullies and hills, to palm groves in some canyons, and even pine-covered heights. The valley has many springs, and this underground source is used in Borrego Valley for the cultivation of several thousand acres of land. The desert bighorn sheep, which furnished part of the park's name (*borrego* is Spanish for bighorn sheep), still roam some of its remote areas. Many animal, bird, and insect species are found in this desert. Among the 600 plant varieties here are smoke trees, Washingtonia palms, and elephant trees with their distinctive fat trunks.

Just over the mountains to the west of this desert preserve is an area of great scenic and historical charm within quite a small compass. This is the San Diego "back country," a region to the north and east of California's southern-most coastal city. San Diego, itself, is, of course, a charmer. That theme receives consideration in the part of this commentary devoted to the coast. This hinterland has an equal appeal. It has an unassuming magic that can even captivate the visitor who has been the length and breadth of California and has his senses stretched by all the spectaculars he has encountered in this spectacular state. This time he's in a sometimes gentle, sometimes rugged country, with good

Tehachapi Mountains near Lancaster

Big Sur Coastline

Mount Shasta

The General Grant Giant Sequoia, Kings Canyon National Park

Joshua Tree National Monument

Bridal Veil Falls, Yosemite National Park

Laguna Beach

San Gabriel Mountains

Anza-Borrego Desert State Park

West Fork of Carson River, Sierra Nevada Mountains

Emerald Bay, Lake Tahoe

South Fork of Kings River, Kings Canyon National Park

Big Sur Coastline

Lone Cypress, Seventeen Mile Drive

Autumn in the Sierras near Big Pine

Mission San Carlos Borromeo de Carmelo, Carmel

Sierra Mountains near Lone Pine

Point Lobos State Reserve

Mount Lassen

San Francisco and Golden Gate Bridge

Farming near Garberville

Big Sur

Vernal Falls, Yosemite National Park

Anza-Borrego Desert State Park

Morro Bay and Morro Rock

Monterey Bay

Whipple Mountains

South Monterey Bay

Burney Falls

San Diego

State Capitol Building, Sacramento

Death Valley

Bonita Point Lighthouse

Sabina Lake near Bishop

Bristlecone Pine, Shulman Grove and Sierra Nevada Mountains

Big Sur Coastline

Sunrise in Joshua Tree National Monument

Sunrise at Santa Cruz

Anza-Borrego Desert State Park

Dana Meadows, Yosemite National Park

North of Mendocino

Mono Lake

Santa Cruz Lighthouse

Redwood National Park

Palos Verdes Coastline

Los Angeles

Tuolumne Meadows, Yosemite National Park

Joshua Tree National Monument

backcountry roads to take him through it at a casual pace. Even so, there's a variety of scenery on the menu — meadows, mountains, and even desert. There are plenty of remote areas for hiking, and state parks for camping. Or an overnight stay the old mining town of Julian, in the mountains, might unlock the forgotten secrets of a past era. Julian has changed little from the 1860s, when it had a brief boom as a gold town.

The history of this region is an amalgam of Indian mythology, mission activity, and gold mining. An excellent example of mission restoration is the celebrated Mission San Luis Rey, a little east of Oceanside. Farther along on the same road (State 76) that goes by this mission is the San Antonio de Pala Mission. After this, the road goes through a valley from where the great Palomar Observatory is visible. The turnoff road to Palomar offers magnificent scenery. The observatory, itself, affords visitors a gallery view of its well-known 200-inch Hale telescope. Cuyamaca Rancho State Park, 60 miles from San Diego, has trails for riding and hiking and mountain peaks that look out over the ocean to the west and the desert to the east. There are Indian relics and an old gold mine within the park.

The gentle countryside and slower pace of this part of California have something to impart to the sensitive observer who roams the countryside. Here, one seems to have both a sense of place and of time, an awareness that he "belongs." Identity with one's environment is a rarely-found treasure in these times, becoming harder than ever to experience as man overcrowds his living space and turns it into a kind of nonreality.

The Coast

Reading a map of California is an adventure all by itself, and that long, long coastline is an important part of the story. The ragged Pacific edge measures more than 1,000 miles and stretches from high in the temperate zone into the subtropical. The coastal climates and landscapes rival the interior regions for variety.

The coastal redwood — the tallest tree on earth — once grew in a vast forest almost 500-miles long and 30-miles wide, from south of Monterey into a corner of Oregon. But even this vast distribution represented a retreat, caused by climate and surface changes, from their ubiquitous presence over the northern hemisphere many millions of years ago. The more recent retreat of the redwoods, to scattered groves along the northern California coast, was brought about by the remorseless drive of human civilization. Redwood lumber, most of us are aware, is not only beautiful, but highly disease- and rot-resistant; so before they were protected, the big trees were harvested without regard to the future. The name "Big Trees," by the way, is more commonly applied to the giant Sequoia, which grows in a restricted area of the central Sierra. Both species are redwoods, but the coastal variety *(Sequoia sempervirens)* may attain a height of more than 300 feet, with an average diameter of 10 feet. The Big Trees of the Sierra Nevada *(Sequoiadendron giganteum)* grow 200 to 250 feet high, with a 25-foot diameter. They are the biggest living things on earth (see "The Sierra Nevada" for further comment on the Big Trees).

Redwood National Park, of recent creation (1968), stretches south from Crescent City. Within its 58,000 acres are three state parks: Jedediah Smith, Del Norte, and Prairie Creek. US Highway 101, the "Redwood Highway," runs through these redwood groves as it does through those to the south in Humboldt, Mendocino, and Sonoma counties. To see the best specimens of redwood, the proper procedure is to take to the trails in the groves. Another possibility is a 40-mile ride through redwood country on the "Skunk" or "Super Skunk," two passenger trains that run daily, in season. The latter train is drawn by a steam locomotive.

The rugged north coast gets plenty of rain and fog, making it possible for the redwoods to grow up so big and strong. And that is good from a purely human perspective, because the tourist-seeking coastal towns, like Eureka and Arcata, are happy to receive the multitudes who come from near and far to pay homage to the forest giants. The points on the coast, of course, have their own reasons for being there, too. In Humboldt Bay, which spreads out north and south of Eureka, is an island (Gunther Island) isolated from the man-made establishments around the bay and as a result, is totally unspoiled. One can easily reach it by a small boat from Eureka. Once you get there, watch the abundant bird life, or dig for clams, or just be a part of the scene.

The region of the north coast is an exception to the intense population growth in many parts of the state during the past decades. Now that fishing and logging have declined, the area has fewer human inhabitants than it did when those activities were more important. The towns are quite small — Eureka and Fort Bragg are the only ones of any size — and far apart. The pace and appearance is more like the nineteenth century than the twentieth. Two settlements in particular are notable for their charm, reminiscent of another era: Ferndale, southwest of Eureka, contains many structures of the Victorian period; and Mendocino, a community south of Fort Bragg, is also patterned after New England Victorian architecture. Mendocino has a reputation as an art colony and tourist attraction that belies its small population. The coastal area of Mendocino County displays its rich Victorian background not only in its towns but in the places between the towns. The farms and sheep ranches on which the economy is based have buildings that also look like period pieces.

The north coast wine country of Napa and Sonoma counties contains the major number of California's wineries. Here, in warm valleys where many varieties of grapes can be grown in abundance, the state's celebrated wine producers are clustered. Names like Louis Martini, Charles Krug, Beringer Brothers, and Christian Brothers are located here, and tours are conducted through the wineries. The Napa-Sonoma region is one of the small pockets of California whose scenery is gentle and undramatic. Its unspectacular wooded hills and rich valleys have a very special beauty.

The town of Sonoma in this region has great historical significance. In Sonoma, early in the last century, the Hungarian viticulturist Agoston Haraszthy gave the California wine industry its first impetus by introducing cuttings from European countries. The town is the site of Mission San Francisco Solano do Sonoma and was also the last home of Jack London, the author. The central plaza of Sonoma, restored by the state, is now a museum where mementos, mission relics, documents, and paintings of the early days are preserved. The town contains reminders of California's Mexican heritage, including the home of the Mexican administrator, General Mariano Vallejo. The Jack London State Historic Park is a few miles north of the town.

The Sonoma coastline is quite undeveloped, with wild, awesome scenery provided by the Coast Range's abrupt and swooping plunges down to the ocean. The most famous settlement in this stretch is Fort Ross, now a national monument as well as a state park. Fort Ross contains blockhouses and a commandant's house dating from the time of the nineteenth-century Russian fur traders. The blockhouses, situated on a lofty headland, are all that remain of the original, high-walled stockade of four buildings. The Russian River flows down through the region's Santa Rosa Valley and makes a sharp bend, heading for the coast a little south of Fort Ross. A resort country known as "The River" has grown up in this section between the river's bend and the coast, with Guerneville as its center.

Just north of the San Francisco Bay area is the Point Reyes Peninsula, a large, triangular piece of land whose differences from the surrounding coast are interesting. Its weather is wetter and windier, some of its plant life is unique to the peninsula, and its ridges contain untouched fir forests with giant trees. The Point Reyes Beach is characterized by a long stretch of sand, headlands, and crashing waves. The Point Reyes National Seashore, authorized in 1962, is under development. Close by, in the North Bay area, are the well-known Muir Woods, a stand of virgin coast redwoods set aside as a national monument. In addition to an intimate look at the big trees, the park affords a thrilling view of the Golden Gate from the heights of its canyon wall.

The jewel of the north coast — some say of the *whole Pacific* coast — is San Francisco. It is one of the few really great cities in the world, part of a select number whose unique standing depends not on the size of its population or the extent of its territory (San Francisco is rather small in area and its population is about one million). Its magic comes from many elements, among them its air conditioned weather, tolerant philosophy, up-and-down streets, fascinating architecture, and land-sea ambience. The Queen City by the Bay has to be something special to outshine the many burgeoning communities that line the Bay shores. Oakland is next in line, with some qualities quite as unusual as those of her big sister across the Bay. Oakland has come out of San Francisco's shadow since World War II.

Below the southern end of the Bay is San Jose, a former agricultural center that exploded into an industrial city in the fifties and sixties and is still getting bigger. The Bay shore might be considered one continuous city, except that the three biggest communities and most of the smaller ones, like Los Gatos, Palo Alto, Redwood City, San Mateo, Alameda and Berkeley all have their unique flavor.

Monterey Bay begins about 50 miles south of San Francisco. Its northern end is marked by the city of Santa Cruz, and Monterey Peninsula is on the southern extremity. Santa Cruz is a popular beach town with many man-made and natural attractions associated with developed coastal cities. It makes a good starting place for exploring the beaches of the Bay. Monterey Peninsula, mile-for-mile, possesses one of the most beautiful (and celebrated) shorelines in the world. Its fascination is heightened by the presence of historic Monterey on the north, quiet and quaint Carmel on the south, and the Del Monte Forest in the middle. In Monterey many buildings of the Spanish and Mexican era still stand; the town, itself, is a living museum. Carmel shuns modern, garish trappings and remains, essentially, a village where stores are small and where many crafts are practiced. Many artists live and work in Carmel and display their creations in the downtown galleries. The Del Monte Forest, a private preserve of exclusive homes and exceptional scenery, may be seen by taking the 17-mile drive. Views of Carmel Bay and Pebble Beach, with its famous golf course, are afforded by the drive.

Immediately south of Carmel is the Point Lobos State Reserve, an exceptionally beautiful example of the shaping power of the sea, where it hurls itself against the land. Parts of the shoreline have become deeply indented under the timeless pounding of the ocean. Where the rocks have been strong enough to defy the waves, dark cliffs rise up. The intricate land-sea interplay provides habitat for many species of birds and plants, some rare wildflowers, and a number of wild animals.

About 40 miles farther down the coast, William Randolph Hearst's splendid San Simeon stands like a fairytale castle. A startling example of conspicuous consumption carried to grandiloquent lengths, Hearst's estate overlooks the Pacific from a lofty setting in the Santa Lucia foothills. It is now a state historical monument, and tours are conducted through the priceless collection of magnificent buildings and magnificent art.

One of the pleasant and attractive stopping places along the southern California coast is Morro Bay, a resort and fishing town. Its main feature is enormous Morro Rock, which bulges nearly 600 feet out of the sea just offshore. Nearby to the south is San Luis Obispo, an agricultural center whose first building was the now-famous Mission San Luis Obispo. The Lompoc Valley, just inland over the mountains some 40 miles south of San Luis Obispo, is a riot of color a good part of the year. Here the long rainless summers make conditions ideal for the flower seed growing industry, which produces more than half of the world's supply.

One of the favored cities of the southern coast is Santa Barbara. The coastal mountains (Santa Ynez range) have backed off enough to leave a wide, sheltered, level area for the city. This city, with its Spanish motif, has a beautiful, warm climate all year. The emphasis in Santa Barbara is culture and the environment, rather than commerce. The city's Spanish look is perhaps best exemplified by the Santa Barbara County Court House. Santa Barbara's distance from Los Angeles (95 miles) has saved it from engulfment by that sprawling monster. Its way of life bears scant resemblance to the pace set by the gigantic city-state down the coast.

The long string of beautiful coastal settlements below Los Angeles comes to a glorious finish in San Diego, just above the Mexican border. This city takes pride in her rich Spanish and Mexican heritage. San Diego's Old Town architecture and relaxed way of life are strong reminders of the past. The city is blessed with an enormous, landlocked harbor, which gives it quiet waters for ships from all over the world, and more fine beaches than any other coastal area. The climate is superb all year, cool in summer and warm in winter. The sea breezes keep the air of the city constantly clean and refreshed, even though San Diego is the third largest city on the Pacific Coast. It is called a progressive city by those who know it, a city of the future. This is because San Diego has so successfully blended its historical and natural heritages with its daily life and its plans for the future that its enduring place among the vital communities of the earth is assured.

The Sierra Nevada

The High Sierra is the magnificent climax of the long mountain barrier that covers a large part of eastern California — the Sierra Nevada, the largest unified mountain range in the United States. The western foothills of the granite range reach down into the Sacramento and San Joaquin valleys. The Gold Rush of the last century was concentrated in these foothills, and some of the towns that remain are reminders of that era. The higher elevations are still mostly primitive wilderness rarely visited by man. But some of the jewels in the Sierra crown, because of their ease of access, have become magnets for great multitudes of vacationers in the summer.

The most popular national park in the country is Yosemite, in the central part of the range, visited by several million people each year. By far the greatest number never get beyond the seven-mile Yosemite Valley, a glacial gorge whose sheer walls rise 2,000 to 4,000 feet above a wide, flat floor something like a meadow. The valley cliffs spawn a spectacular array of waterfalls. The highest of these is Yosemite Falls, a free-falling cascade that drops 2,565 feet. Pine and oaks, many kinds of flowers, and grasses grow on the valley floor. Some of the great pinnacles of awesome aspect are El Capitan, Cathedral Rocks, North Dome, Half Dome and Three Brothers.

It's rather a shame that most of the public never gets beyond the narrow confines of the valley. Above it are 1,200 square miles of mountain wilderness with trail that beckon the hiker or horseback rider. John Muir, the famed Sierra Club naturalist whose missionary work on the need for preservation of the wilderness led to the establishment of the national park system, would be somewhat dismayed by the effect over-visiting has had on some areas of the Sierra.

Indeed, the John Muir Trail is one of those that takes off right at the edge of Yosemite valley and plunges into the heart of the mountains. It leads south for 212 miles into Sequoia National Park, ending on the summit of Mount Whitney, the highest peak in the 48-contiguous states (14,495 feet).

Sequoia and Kings Canyon national parks are almost as popular as Yosemite. They, too, enclose more than a thousand square miles of rugged mountains, lakes and streams, but most visitors never get far beyond their portals. Without too much effort they can see what brought them here — the Big Trees, *Sequoiadendron giganteum*, the largest living things in the world. The colossal trees are native only to the western slopes of the Sierras and mostly in the middle and southern parts of the range. Sequoia and Kings Canyon have the biggest trees, some of whose groves are easily accessible by car or a short trail hike. The Big Trees, whose bark is cinnamon red with shades of gray, are cousins of the coastal redwoods. Over a long life span that may be several thousand years, they reach heights above 250 feet and an average diameter of 25 feet. Some groves of these giants are not easily accessible, a happy guarantee of their survival in the early lumbering days, as well as now, during these latter-day mass pilgrimages into their domain.

Directly across the Sierra from Sacramento is the immensely popular vacation area, Lake Tahoe. The lake is 22-miles long and up to 12-miles wide, surrounded by densely wooded mountains. The deep blue waters of Tahoe attract boaters, water skiers, and even swimmers, although the water is cold. The lake can be visited in summer or winter. Wintertime activities come alive at Lake Tahoe and the surrounding area, which includes the Tahoe Basin, with a multitude of snow activities, from downhill and cross-country skiing, to snow-mobiling, sledding, and other family-oriented snow fun.

The survival of the high country as wilderness is quite remarkable in view of the centers of dense population not far away. One reason is simple: it's too rugged for easy access. The mountains line up on the east side of the state for 400 miles north to south. In the winter nearly all of the relatively few roads over it are closed by snow, making entrance from the east an uncertain affair. In the early days of movement into California, the white man was simply helpless before the fearsome mountain barrier in the wintertime. Fremont made it across in the winter of 1844 but not without incredible hardship and starvation. During that journey the blizzard-bound party had to slaughter and eat most of its animals. And Fremont chose the relatively gentle elevations south of Lake Tahoe for his crossing. Three years later George Donner led a group of emigrants across the pass that now bears his name. Many of them perished, and diaries of the party tell the grisly story of what some of the survivors were forced to dine on.

The accident of geology, however, is only one reason the Sierra has not been trampled into extinction. The range's eight national forests and three enormous national parks have enfolded huge areas within their protective embrace. In the national forests, 939,000 acres of the high country have been designated as Wilderness, where man may only visit and never alter. This state of affairs was decreed by Congress in the Wilderness Act of 1964.

Death Valley and the Mojave Desert

Surely one of the best-known places on the earth's face is Death Valley. It has become legendary by reason of some features that distinguish it from other desert areas. Now a national monument, the valley stretches north and south for almost 100 miles on the eastern edge of Southern California. It is a place of extremes, even more so than the vast Mojave Desert to the south. One of these extremes is expressed in its temperatures, probably the hottest anywhere in the world in summer (134° was recorded in 1913). The summer temperature may remain at 100 all night long in the desert lowlands, while cooling off considerably on the surrounding mountains that are also part of the desert environment. Another superlative for which Death Valley is known concerns its elevation. Some 14-square miles are more than 280 feet below sea level; near the valley's center is a place called Badwater, at 282 feet below sea level, the lowest point in the Western Hemisphere. Telescope Peak, nearby, is a startling contrast: it towers 11,049 feet into the desert skies.

Death Valley has an undeserved reputation as a place that reaped a fearful toll of the mid-nineteenth-century pioneers who crossed it. Only one "forty-niner" is known to have died on the journey through the desert, and he expired from causes other than heat or thirst. A little later on, as the Gold Rush grew more frenzied, many of those heading for the gold fields did, indeed, fall victim to the desert's harsh atmosphere.

Of importance to geologists is Death Valley's value as a kind of natural time capsule. It has yielded fossils of prehistoric animals, showing that at some period it was a fertile plain whose climate gradually became drier and whose granite rocks were gradually worn down by the wind and turned into the sand dunes that now cover much of the valley floor. There are lots of rocks left in the

2,000,000 acres of Death Valley. According to students of geology, the rocks of all the divisions of geologic time are represented in earthquake-created folds and blocks several miles thick.

Far from being a lifeless expanse of sand, Death Valley supports a wide and unique variety of plant life. The flora have adapted to the desert environment with specialized root and leaf systems. High on Telescope Peak grow the earth's oldest living things, the bristlecone pines. Most of the valley's animals move about only at night, searching for food. They, too, have adapted to desert conditions, creating moisture from their food.

Below Death Valley, filling up southeastern California and southern Nevada, is the vast Mojave Desert. This is high-desert land varying from 2,000 to 11,000 feet. Understandably, with these different elevations, several kinds of terrain make up the Mojave. Much of it is wild and rugged but much of it has lost its standing as a wilderness retreat. Many cities and towns have developed in places where settlement is possible and modern roads run over a great deal of the Mojave, linking up the places of human habitation. Wildlife is no longer as abundant as it once was.

From the point of view of comfort, and visual rewards, the best time to visit the Mojave is during the period February through May. In early and late spring, desert wildflowers are on brilliant display. Gilians and desert primroses are common desert blooms. A variety of mariposa usually adorns the western rim of the Mojave in late spring with its orange-chrome petals and purple anthers. The Mojave aster, with big lilac blooms on graceful stems, grows in the gravelly earth of the mesas and on the rocky hills. The purple lupine covers stretches of the interior, along with the lemon and green caulanthus stalks.

The town of Apple Valley is in one of the developed areas of the Mojave. It is part of the western reach of the desert, with the Mojave River running along the west and the San Bernardino foothills delineating its southern border. Once a dwelling place of the Indians, it is now a resort community with all the trappings essential to the pleasure of visitors in such places. Just north of Apple Valley, at Victorville, Interstate 15 freeway begins its run across the mid-northern Mojave. A back road taking off from the freeway at Victorville parallels the Mojave River for many miles and returns to the main highway at Barstow. During its run this side road passes through rural beauty spots and ranches near the river, and some tiny villages. Along the way are quite a few deserted buildings. Beyond Barstow is the ghost town of Calico, an old silver mining town founded in 1881. Its attraction for tourists has brought it back to life.

From Barstow Interstate 15 shoots straight for the Nevada border and Interstate 40 angles in a south-easterly direction toward Arizona. For the serious desert-watcher, both of these roads can serve as feeders into some fascinating scenery. A hiker (with canteen) can take off on a short hike from the end of a five-mile side road 30 miles east of Barstow into the heart of beautiful Afton Canyon, whose fluted pink cliffs rise up from the sand and the Mojave River. Farther east, around Baker, are deserted ranches and mines, with their abandoned buildings adding a touch of pathos to the scene. The hills at this spot provide a good view across Soda Lake (dry).

Interstate 40 — the southeast road — pushes around low desert mountains. Eight miles after Barstow is Daggett, a pioneer town that maintains as a museum a blacksmith shop where borax wagons were built. About one-third of the way along I-40, at Ludlow, US Highway 66 takes a side trip to four desert communities before joining the freeway, again, just past Essex. About two miles from the paved road at Amboy is the 200-foot-high volcanic Amboy Crater, whose interior may be seen after a 10-minute climb. A 70-mile unpaved but graded road from Amboy to Baker (on I-15) allows the desert explorer to get closer to his subject.

Northwest of Essex, in the Providence Mountains, is the Mitchell Caverns State Reserve, featuring a system of limestone caves situated about 1,000 feet above the desert floor. A nature trail and a visitor center with a panoramic view of the desert are also part of the reserve.

The upper Mojave area provides a great deal of diversity. Its western corner, bordered by the converging Tehachapi and San Gabriel ranges, is almost pastoral. This is Antelope Valley, where it is possible to grow plants from non-desert areas. The northwestern Mojave is more generally a land of harsh contrasts. The southern Sierras rise to great heights in the west but low, dry lakes are spotted over much of the northwestern interior. Human history is now written into much of this desert's story. First the Indians left their traces, with markings on rocks; later, the mines and mining towns remained in the desert to tell of a different culture.

In spite of the intrusion of civilization into the Mojave in this century, a desert-watcher can't help feeling that it's all part of the desert's unchanging change. Just like the Indian markings and the miners' towns, the artifacts of technological civilization may one day be just another sign in the desert that another culture passed this way.